6470

Going Green

by Kris Hirschmann

ERICKSON PRESS

Yankton, South Dakota

ERICKSON PRESS

© 2008 Erickson Press

For more information, contact
Erickson Press
329 Broadway
PO Box 33
Yankton, SD 57078

Or you can visit our Internet site at www.ericksonpress.com

LIBRARY OF CONGRESS CATALOGING-IN-PUBLICATION DATA

Hirschmann, Kris, 1967–
  Going green / by Kris Hirschmann.
     p. cm. — (Ripped from the headlines)
  Includes bibliographical references and index.
Summary: This high-interest book for low-reading-level students examines climate change, how people have contributed to global warming, and measures being taken to address the problem. Topics discussed include reducing pollution, saving energy, using "green" products, reducing waste, and developing cleaner energy sources.
  ISBN: 978-1-60217-025-4 (hardcover : alk. paper)
  1. Environmental protection—Citizen participation—Juvenile literature. I. Title.
  TD171.7.H57 2008
  333.72—dc22

                                                          2007043701

Printed in the United States of America

Contents

Why Go Green?

Most restaurants sell bottled water. In 2007, though, an eatery called Chez Panisse took this drink off the menu. "For us, it's about doing the right thing," says general manager Michael Kossa-Rienzi. "If people really understood what was behind the manufacture of those plastic bottles, they would think twice."[1]

Kossa-Rienzi is referring to the fact that making, filling, and shipping water bottles burns oil. Also, the used bottles end up in landfills. Tap water, on the other hand, is nearly pollution-free. So by serving tap water, Chez Panisse is doing one small thing to help the Earth.

Environmentalists have a phrase that describes this type of act. They call it "going green." Going green simply means making Earth-friendly choices. Turning off unused lights, for instance, is a green act. So is walking to the store or buying chemical-free foods. These choices are green because they save energy and reduce pollution. If everyone did these simple things, the Earth's environment would be healthier than it is today.

Unfortunately, everyone does not do these things. But today more and more people are trying. They realize that it is important to take care of

Alice Waters, owner of Chez Panisse, urges people to use tap water.

the Earth. "We only have one planet," says a man named Jeff. "If we waste it or spoil it, we put ourselves in a great deal of trouble."[2]

Jeff and others like him are leading a green revolution. They are trying to be kind to the environment. They hope that others will follow their example. When enough people go green, everyone—including Mother Earth—will reap the rewards.

Chapter 1

Going Green at Home

A woman named Ruth loves to send Christmas cards to her friends. Ruth does not buy new cards each year. Instead, she has found a way to reuse old ones. "I tear off the front section of the cards I receive, and send them out postcard style to my friends the following year. This way, I don't need to buy cards and envelopes," she explains. "I'm saving trees, and the people I've talked to really appreciate it."[3]

Like many people, Ruth is trying to make greener choices. She knows that reusing Christmas cards will not save the planet. But she also knows that going green is not always about big actions. It means taking small steps as well. By making good choices at home, individuals can help the Earth to be a better place.

Reduce, Reuse, Recycle

Reducing waste, as Ruth does, is an easy first step toward going green. With practice, it can even

An Inconvenient Truth

People once thought going green was for hippies. But a documentary called *An Inconvenient Truth* helped to change this idea. In this film, former U.S. vice president Al Gore talks about the Earth's climate. He shows evidence that humans are making the Earth warmer. He says it is critical to stop this trend. He also makes it clear that every person can and should help.

Gore's film was a surprise hit. It won many awards, including the 2006 Academy Award for Best Documentary Feature. It was seen by millions of people. Many of these people were shocked by Gore's words. Some even started making greener choices as a result. "I did a funny thing when I came home after seeing [this movie]. I went around the house turning off the lights," wrote film critic Roger Ebert in one review.

Roger Ebert is not the only person who liked Gore's film. The Nobel committee was impressed, too. In October 2007, the committee awarded Gore the Nobel Peace Prize for his world-changing efforts.

Former vice president Al Gore speaks often about global warming.

Roger Ebert, "*An Inconvenient Truth*," Robert Ebert.com, June 2, 2006. http://rogerebert.suntimes.com/apps/pbcs.dll/article?AID=/20060601/REVIEWS/60517002/1023.

A teen collects a pile of newspapers for recycling.

become a way of life. "I think about how everything I buy might end up in a landfill. . . . We don't buy anything disposable, not even napkins. It's just about being aware of the choices made in the grocery store and anywhere else we shop,"[4] says a woman named Amie.

Not everyone is as dedicated as Amie. Most people buy at least some disposable goods. These goods, however, do not always need to be thrown away. They can often be recycled instead. Aluminum, glass, paper, and plastics, for instance, can be taken to recycling centers. There they are broken down and made into new goods. These goods are considered green because they use old materials instead of fresh ones.

Recycling things is just a start. Buying them again in their new form is the next step. Recycled napkins,

The Bride Wore . . . Green?

Many engaged couples worry about the environment. These couples often try to make their weddings as green as possible. They may print their invitations on recycled paper. They may order organic food and flowers. Some couples even buy recycled rings. These choices do not erase a wedding's impact on the environment. But they do reduce it. "Our goal is to plan an event that is as light on the Earth as possible," says a groom-to-be named Ryan.

Ryan's fiancée, Carla, explains her thoughts a bit further. "It's not just about the wedding for us. It's about how we are going to live after the wedding," she explains. "We want our wedding to symbolize what our marriage is going to be about."

Quoted in Janet Kornblum, "The Bride's in Green," *USA Today*, June 25, 2007, section D, page 1.

bath tissue, and other products are not expensive. They are also easy to find. Using them can make a big difference. A group called the Natural Resources Defense Council claims that 544,000 trees would be saved if every American household bought just one roll of recycled paper towels.

Composting

Manufactured products are not the only source of household waste. Food also creates garbage. Coffee grounds, carrot peels, and other foods wind up in people's trash cans every day. This type of waste makes up 20 to 30 percent of the material found in landfills.

Food waste cannot be recycled like paper or glass. In other words, it cannot be made into new food. It can, however, be changed into dirt. To make this change happen, a person tosses food scraps onto an outdoor pile. Natural processes break the scraps down over time. They eventually turn into rich soil. This process is called composting, and it is practiced in many green homes.

Workers with an organic farming organization in Africa tend to a large compost pile.

Many people are passionate about composting. They point out that it is simple and effective. "Creating compost is one of the easiest and best things everyone can do to help the environment," explains a woman named Maribeth. "I am creating it in my own yard and not passing on my waste. . . . In my small way, I'm doing what I can to help our world."[5]

Organic Eating

Compost is even better, of course, if it is made from chemical-free scraps. Foods that contain no pesticides or hormones are called organics. They are con-

Whole Foods and many other markets sell organic foods.

sidered green because they have little lasting impact on the Earth. Many people think they are healthier, fresher, and tastier than regular foods as well. For all of these reasons, organics are becoming more and more popular. They are sold today at farmers' markets, green grocery stores like Whole Foods, and even regular groceries.

There is one issue with organic foods. Growing them takes extra time and care. Organics therefore tend to cost more than regular foods. Some people solve this problem by joining organic co-ops. Others grow their own fruits and vegetables. Most, though, just pay the price. "It does cost a bit more, true, but the peace of mind you get from knowing you're not pumping chemicals into your body makes up for that,"[6] says a shopper named Kate.

Other Organics

Foods are just one type of organic product. People can also buy organic clothes and health care items. They can choose green bedding, furniture, and countless other things as well. These products are at least as good as nonorganics. They are also widely available. As a result, many people shop green in all areas of their lives.

Major retailers have noticed this trend. Some are reacting by creating organic product lines. Levi Strauss, for instance, launched a line of all-organic "Eco" jeans in the fall of 2006. Nike sells many organic items. So do sportswear giant Patagonia and boot maker Timberland. Like organic food, these

goods can be expensive. But many people are glad to spend the extra money. "The price is well worth it. Buying organic cotton makes the world a safer, cleaner place,"[7] explains one consumer.

Many people feel the same way about green cosmetics. Today stores everywhere stock organic shampoos, lotions, and more. A few popular stores, including the Body Shop, carry nothing *but* all-natural items. With so many options, it is no wonder green beauty products are becoming more popular.

Greening Your Cleaning

Green cleaning is yet another hot topic among home-owners. Studies show that indoor air can be five times more polluted than outdoor air. Fumes from cleaning products cause much of this pollution. By using natural products instead of dangerous chemicals, people can cut down on these fumes.

Characteristics of Green Cleaning Products

No ozone-depleting substances
Packaging can be recycled
Recycled content in packaging
Less likely to catch fire
Dyes reduced or not added, except for safety purposes
Fragrances reduced or not added
Skin irritants reduced or not added
Less packaging

Source: www.epa.gov/epp/pubs/products/cleaning.htm.

Some people support totally natural cleaning. They claim that water, vinegar, and baking soda will take care of any mess. This approach does work. However, it can be slow. As one homeowner explains, "When cleaning the oven with, say, baking soda, you have to let it work while you sleep." She is quick to point out that she does not see this as a bad thing. "Isn't that what we're after, anyway?"[8] she jokes.

Not everyone is this patient. For faster results, many people count on green cleaning products to keep their homes fresh. Green cleaners are chemi-

Danny Seo, the "Green Martha Stewart"

When Danny Seo was a teenager, he had a brainstorm. "Why can't green be beautiful? Why can't it be fun?" he thought. Seo started coming up with clever green ideas anyone could do at home. In the process, he became famous. Now 30 years old, Seo has written many books and articles about green living. He has hosted his own TV series, *Simply Green with Danny Seo*. He is also a regular guest on many other shows. Endlessly inventive, Seo is sometimes called the "green Martha Stewart." He is living proof that when it comes to going green, one person really can make a difference.

Quoted in Anh-Minh Le, "The Next Martha Stewart Is Young, Green and a Guy," *San Francisco Chronicle*, November 1, 2006, p. HO-1.

cals, not natural substances. But they do not contain ammonia, bleach, and other common toxins. As a result, they are nearly fume free. This means they do not pollute the air like traditional cleaners.

Today green cleaners have moved into the mainstream. They are being used in homes and businesses everywhere. According to Denny YoungeDyke, maintenance director of the Petoskey, Michigan, school district, cleaning green is an easy choice. "It's just a matter of using healthier products for the students and the staff. They clean just as well, they're cost effective, and there's no reason not to do it,"[9] he says.

Be an Energy Miser

Most people use green cleaners for health reasons. The choice to conserve energy, though, is all about protecting the environment. Electricity is usually made by burning oil, gas, and coal. This process creates pollution. Saving electricity, therefore, helps to save the Earth as well.

Low-energy appliances are one tool for going green. Green appliances do the same jobs as standard ones. However, they use less power. This means they are better for the environment. In the United States, green appliances bear a blue Energy Star logo. This logo makes it very easy for consumers to shop green.

Energy-saving lightbulbs can also make a difference. Compact fluorescent lightbulbs (CFLs) burn much less power than regular bulbs. They cost a bit more, but they save money in the long run.

Energy-Saving Lightbulbs

One CFL per household would save 90 billion pounds (40.8 billion kg) of greenhouse gas emissions.

Compact fluorescent lightbulb (CFL)

This is equal to taking 7.5 million cars off the road.

Source: www.environment.about.com/od/greenlivingdesign/a/light_bulbs.htm?p=1.

Over its lifetime, one CFL can cut up to $30 off a home's electric bill.

For real savings, of course, people do not need to buy special lightbulbs or appliances. They just need to burn less energy. Turning off unused lights is one way to do this. People can also use less air-conditioning and unplug idle appliances. They can even focus on smaller details. In Karen's home, for instance, "We put lids on pans when boiling water [and] don't overfill the kettle." Karen knows that these things only save a tiny bit of power. But a tiny bit is better than nothing. "I know simple changes can make a difference,"[10] she explains. By greening her home, Karen is doing her part to help the Earth.

Chapter 2

Building Green

A man named Bryan believes in green living. To him this does not mean turning off a few lightbulbs. It means being in harmony with the natural world. "The environment isn't just outside. It's what is inside your carpeting, wood, cabinetry and plaster,"[11] he explains.

In 2002 Bryan decided to build a house that lived up to this idea. The result was a green dream. Bryan's Arizona home is made with organic materials. It gets most of its power from the sun. It boasts low-energy appliances and lightbulbs. Some rooms do not even have regular ceilings and walls. They are surrounded by vines and drapes instead. "When you see a bobcat racing across the [nearby] mountain you feel like you should have more of a barrier, but for us it is liberating,"[12] Bryan laughs.

Bryan's home may be extreme. The ideas behind it, however, are not. People today realize that buildings have a big impact on the natural world. They are finding ways to reduce this impact. Homes,

skyscrapers, and everything in between are now being designed with the environment in mind.

Green Materials

A green building starts with green materials. A green material is anything with a low impact on the Earth. Hemp, bamboo, cotton, and cork, for instance, can be grown organically. They also grow very quickly. In other words, they are renewable. Renewable goods are always greener than factory-made products such as glass and metal.

Recycled materials are also considered green. Recycled materials might include wood, tiles, and rocks from torn-down buildings. A builder might also reuse old carpets, windows, or other things. By giving these items a second life, builders keep them from going into landfills. They also keep new products from being manufactured. For these reasons, recycled goods are always a green choice.

To date, no modern building has been made of green materials alone. But some come close. The Ranch House at Del Sur, California, is one amazing

LEEDing the Way

The U.S. Green Building Council has come up with a rating system for green buildings. The system is called Leadership in Energy and Environmental Design. It is usually called LEED for short. LEED lays out goals for green construction. Buildings are rated according to how many goals they meet.

A building does not have to be LEED certified to be green. For green rookies, though, LEED can be a good planning tool. "I pushed for LEED to be used on [a] project because it gave us a blueprint for greening a building," explains one builder. "Without a standard to follow, we would have had some green aspects but limited consistency and quality."

Quoted in Alana Klein, "Green Expectations," *University Business*, February 2005, p. 50.

example of green construction. The floors of this building are made from old barn planks. The ceiling beams were plucked from a torn-down pier. The chimney and fireplaces are built from local rocks. The floors are cork, and the kitchen counters are made of sunflower seeds. The seeds are ground up and then pressed into hard slabs.

In one interview, Del Sur executive Bill Dumka talks about planning the Ranch House. He recalls that no one knew quite what to do at first. They thought it would be hard to build green. But they

To help Hurricane Katrina victims, actor Brad Pitt is involved in building 150 "green" homes in New Orleans.

The Cost of Going Green

Building green can be pricey. Adding just a few green features tacks 2 to 4 percent onto the cost of a home. Extreme greening might add 30 percent or more.

Many homeowners, however, are happy to pay this price. "If you're building a house as a lifelong investment, it just seems like the right thing to do," says a man named Jason. It can also lead to long-term savings. "Our friends' energy bills were almost double ours last winter," Jason notes.

Quoted in Sarah Max, "It's Easy Being Green," *Money*, January 2007, p. 51.

soon discovered it was not hard at all. In fact, it was easy. "We just kept adding on things that didn't seem to be a big burden," [13] Dumka says. The result was one of the world's greenest buildings.

No Toxins Allowed

A truly green building is not just good for the Earth. It is good for the people inside it, too. Today there are many choices when it comes to planning healthy buildings.

Choosing nontoxic products is one important part of the plan. Why? Many traditional building materials contain chemicals called volatile organic compounds (VOCs). Over time, VOCs escape into the air as fumes. This process is called off-gassing, and it can make people very sick. A woman named

Drey had this experience when she was house hunting. "After about ten minutes I started to get a horrible headache that lasted the rest of the evening. The owner of the house said she had [recently] painted the inside," [14] Drey explains.

To avoid problems like this, builders can choose low- or no-VOC paints and stains. These materials do not give off fumes. This means they do not pollute the air inside a building. They work well and look great. They are also widely available. Home improvement store Lowe's, for instance, sells zero-VOC paint in more than a thousand shades. Home Depot sells a similar line under its Eco Options brand. These products cost about the same as regular paints. Using them is therefore an easy choice for any green builder.

But why stop there? There are many low-VOC products besides paint and stain. A company called American Clay sells VOC-free plaster. A natural flooring product called Marmoleum is greener than fume-filled linoleum. Dozens of low-VOC glues are now on the market. There are nontoxic carpets, caulks, and wallpapers. Really green builders can even insulate walls with shredded blue jeans instead of VOC-laden fiberglass. These products make any building a healthier place.

Saving Energy

Energy choices can also make a building greener. Traditional homes waste a lot of power. This problem is hard to solve once a building is fin-

Solar power supplies the energy needs for this house.

ished. At the design stage, however, it is very easy to address. There are many ways for builders to plan an energy-efficient building.

Basic design features can greatly reduce a building's power needs. In hot climates, for instance, a home can face away from direct sunlight. This keeps the home cooler, which means it needs less air-conditioning. Tinted windows can do the same job. So can carefully placed trees and bushes. Even paint color makes a difference. Light colors reflect more sunlight than dark colors do. In warm regions, therefore, a white house will stay cooler than a brown one. Details like this create automatic, or passive, power savings. They are a key part of any green building plan.

The next step is finding ways to cut waste. Green buildings usually have airtight windows and air ducts to prevent leaks. They may have skylights or other natural lighting methods. They use the greenest appliances on the market. They may even watch people's power usage. A dorm at the University of South Carolina, for instance, has motion sensors in every room. The sensors turn off the lights when people are not present.

As a final step, builders can consider green power sources. Wind and sunlight are the most popular green sources. Hydrogen, landfill gas, and ground heat are other options. These resources are Earth

Workers put down the top floor ceiling of a new green office building.

friendly because they never run out. They do not create pollution. They are also free once solar panels or other collection devices have been installed. By using green power, a building can cut its electric bills to almost nothing.

A man named John can vouch for this fact. He boasts that his wind turbine "provides more than half of our electricity—and when it's windy, nearly all of it." As a result, John and his wife now base their power use on the weather. "We check to see if it's windy before we put on the dishwasher or washing machine,"[15] he says.

Green Chic

A green home can be a chic home. Here are just a few of the trendy green products on the market today.

- Caroma dual-flush toilets have two water tanks. One tank holds 0.8 gallons (3L) of water. The other holds 1.6 gallons (6L). The tanks flush separately. Users choose which tank to use, according to the amount of waste. This helps to save water. Price: $399.
- Scrapile benches are made of glued-together wood scraps. Turning these scraps into useful items keeps them from going into landfills. Price: $754.
- The Skystream personal windmill makes power when the wind blows. In breezy regions, this gadget can cut a home's electric bill in half. Price: $8,000.

Low-Impact Living

Saving power is important. The greenest buildings, however, go much further than that. They are designed to save many other resources as well.

Water is one of these resources. In some buildings, used water from sinks, showers, and toilets flows into special collection systems. These systems treat the water to remove germs and solid waste. The treated liquid is used to flush toilets and water gardens. The same water can be captured and reused over and over again. This prevents it from flowing into sewers and becoming a burden on the environment.

Rainwater, too, can be put to good use. Some buildings have tanks on their roofs to collect this resource. The collected water is filtered and sterilized. It then becomes part of the building's main water supply. In wet places, rainwater can fill most of a building's water needs.

Buildings do not just use water, of course. They also change the way it reaches the Earth in the first place. To reduce this effect, some buildings have plant-covered roofs. These turf or "veggie" roofs absorb rain. During storms, they keep water from pouring off the building and washing soil away. Turf roofs also create a place for insects, birds, and

The bubble-shaped roof of a new aquatic center in China will recycle rainwater.

other small creatures to live. These roofs return oxygen to the air. They even save energy by blocking most of the sun's rays. Cooler buildings use less air-conditioning, which means less power as well.

In a 2005 interview, student Tim Carter talks about a turf roof he created at the University of Georgia. "Roofs are often considered unusable space. But roofs actually provide an ideal green space," he says. Besides, he points out, "I don't know many people who would rather look at gravel." [16]

With this comment, Carter raises a good point. Traditional buildings are not just bad for the Earth. They can be hard on the eyes, too. Features like turf roofs help by bringing a hint of green into cities. They also remind people of the natural world around them. In the process, they encourage people to think green.

Chapter 3

Getting Around in Green Style

Architect Kelley Howell gets on her bicycle each morning. She rides about 8 miles (12.9km) to a bus stop. She then boards a bus that takes her another 16 miles (25.7km) to work. At the end of the day, she makes the same trip in reverse. In all, Kelley buses 32 miles (51.5km) and pedals 16 miles (25.7km) each weekday.

Kelley has a car. It would be much easier for her to drive to work. But Kelley knows that cars create a lot of pollution. She feels that riding bikes and buses is better for the environment. She admits that she is not making a big difference with her actions. However, she says, "If you're not doing something and the next family isn't doing anything, then who will?" [17]

These words sum up a growing attitude toward green travel. People realize that they cannot have a huge impact on their own. Still, they know that each effort counts. They are anxious to do their part. As a result, people today are finding many ways to travel in green style.

Green Rock 'n' Roll

Members of the rock group Barenaked Ladies (BNL) care about the Earth. So when the band tours, it goes in green style. BNL's eight tour buses run on B20. This is a blend of 20 percent biofuel and 80 percent diesel. By using this fuel, the band kept huge amounts of pollution out of the air on its 2006 tour.

BNL singer Steven Page discussed the band's efforts in a 2007 interview. "It is more expensive, but I think it's worth it in the end. . . . I wouldn't do the touring we're doing if we weren't trying to take care of the good part," he said.

Quoted in Linda McAvoy, "Barenaked Ladies Go for the Green," *Toronto Star*, February 3, 2007, p. G01.

The rock group Barenaked Ladies uses special buses for concert tours.

Get Out of the Car

Avoiding cars is the simplest way to go green. Like Kelley, many people bike to work, stores, and other places. Scooters, skateboards, and even feet can also carry a person from place to place. "I always walk

to the local stores even though it takes me 30 minutes rather than a 5-minute drive," [18] explains a man
named Steve.

Walking and other low-speed methods are not
practical for long trips. Sometimes people need
motor vehicles to get around. With a little effort,
however, they can still keep things green. They can
ride buses, subways, trains, or other types of public transport. They can also carpool. This means
sharing a ride with several people. Public vehicles
and shared cars still create pollution. But the impact
is much less than it would be if everyone drove by
themselves.

Cities try to lessen
traffic with special
lanes for car pools.

In some cities, people can take things a step further by joining car clubs. Club members borrow a car whenever they need one. They pay an hourly rate that includes gas, insurance, and repairs. Members still create pollution when they drive. Studies show, however, that car club members drive less than car owners do. In Chicago, for instance, each member of car club I-GO drives about 500 miles (805km) per year. Car owners in the same area drive about 10,000 miles (16,090km) per year.

Cleaner Fuels

Driving less is not the only way to reduce pollution. Car owners can also choose cleaner fuels to run their cars. Clean fuels, or biofuels, are made from plants. Biofuels do give off chemicals when they burn. However, plants took these chemicals from the air very recently. Also, the chemicals would return to the air as soon as the plants died. They are still part of the Earth's natural balance. Fossil fuels, on the other hand, contain chemicals that were taken from the air millions of years ago. These chemicals are no longer part of the Earth's natural balance. When they are released, therefore, they have a huge impact on the planet. For this reason, biofuels are considered greener than fossil fuels.

A liquid called ethanol is the most common biofuel. Ethanol is usually made from corn, wheat, or sugarcane. It can be used on its own. Usually, however, it is mixed with regular gas. Standard mixtures

Eco-travel

Green travel is a hot trend in the tourism industry. To go green, travelers should start by using the cleanest transportation they can find. One Web site offers this advice: "Because planes use so much fuel for take-offs and landings, [you should avoid] planes for trips less than 625 miles (1,006 km). Cars are also major polluters, so your best bet is to take a train or a bus."

Once travelers arrive, they should walk wherever they can. "It's good exercise, great for seeing the sights, and it reduces [the] use of gasoline. Best of all, it's free!" says the same site.

Quoted in Rachel Anderson, "Going Green: Top Ten Rules of Eco-travel," *E: The Environment Magazine*, July/August 2006, p. 52.

include E20 (20 percent ethanol, 80 percent gas) and E85 (85 percent ethanol, 15 percent gas). All U.S.-sold cars can run on E20. With a few engine changes, most can run on E85 as well.

Biodiesel is another common green fuel. This liquid is made from vegetable oil or animal fat. It is so similar to mineral diesel that trucks can use it straight. Like ethanol, however, biodiesel is usually mixed with regular fuel.

In Europe, 5 percent biodiesel (B5) is sold at most gas stations. It is widely used because it is so easy to get. Biodiesel and other green fuels are harder to find in the United States. But this situation may change soon. The state of Oregon, for instance, is working to make E10 and B20 standard at all gas

Biodiesel is loaded for transport in Vermont.

stations. The city of San Francisco uses biodiesel in 40 percent of its trucks. Other cities and states are using biofuels in other ways. This trend will continue as biofuels become more and more common.

Hybrid Vehicles

If using clean fuels is good, using less fuel is even better. One easy way to cut fuel use is to drive a hybrid car. Hybrids get their power from both gas and batteries. The more battery power a car uses, the less gas it burns. Hybrids therefore need much less fuel than regular cars. As a result, they do not create as much pollution.

Buyers today can choose among many hybrid options. One popular car is the Toyota Prius. This vehicle goes about 46 miles (74km) on 1 gallon

(3.8L) of gas. It is the most fuel-efficient car sold in the United States. Other choices include the Camry Hybrid, Honda Accord Hybrid, Ford Escape Hybrid, and many others. In 2006 nearly 250,000 hybrids were sold in the United States alone.

Hybrids are not just good for the Earth. They are good for people's wallets, too. They do cost a bit more to buy, but the gas savings usually make up for it. A typical hybrid owner saves $700 each year on fuel.

Saving money, though, is not the main point for most hybrid buyers. A Prius owner named Tom explains why. "[The Prius] seemed like the most environmentally friendly option out there. . . . I thought it [was] important to put my money where my beliefs are, even if it costs a little more,"[19] he says.

Electric Cars

Some car owners are even more dedicated than Tom. They do not want to use any fuel at all. For these people, electric cars may be a good option. These cars run on battery power alone. With a full battery, they can run about 50 miles (80km). After that the cars are plugged into a wall socket. They take anywhere from a few minutes to a few hours to recharge.

Electric cars do not give off exhaust fumes. However, they are not pollution free. Coal and other fossil fuels are burned to make electricity. So recharging an electric car does affect the Earth.

Studies show, however, that electric cars cause only about half as much pollution as regular cars. For this reason, they are considered a green choice.

Electric cars are not practical for long trips. But they are very good for everyday use. As actor Ed Begley Jr. explains, "Eighty percent of [all] trips are 40 miles (64 km) or less. Well, any electric car can do that, and then some. There's always a way to make it work." Begley should know. He drives his own electric car everywhere he goes. "I'm trying to behave in a way that has less and less of an impact,"[20] he says.

This tiny electric car can travel up to 40 miles before needing to be recharged.

It seems that many other people feel the same way. In 2006 Tesla Motors introduced an electric sports car called the Roadster. One hundred vehicles were built. At a cost of $100,000, these cars were anything but cheap. Still, they all sold immediately. Based on this success, Tesla planned to build 800 Roadsters in 2008. By July 2007 nearly 600 of these cars had been reserved. Current or future owners include California governor Arnold Schwarzenegger, actors George Clooney and Matt Damon, and musicians Flea and will.i.am.

Other Transportation

Cars are a big issue in the green movement. But they are far from the only one. Many types of vehicles can be greener. City buses, for instance, can use biofuels or hybrid engines. Indeed, a 2007 survey showed that many already do. Nearly three-quarters of the cities surveyed have found ways to make city fleets greener.

The news is not as good when it comes to planes, trains, and boats. These vehicles create a great deal of pollution. No easy fixes can make them greener. But some organizations are trying. General Electric's Ecomagination branch, for instance, is now designing green engines for all of these vehicles. NASA is also working on green airplane engines. "Air quality affects everyone right here on Earth, and our program will help,"[21] says a NASA spokesperson.

Japan's new hybrid train runs on diesel fuel and electricity.

Today many companies are following General Electric's and NASA's lead. Business leaders care about the environment. They also see that people are looking for greener options. They want to sell cars, trucks, and other vehicles to these people. Going green therefore helps them to make money. It is a good situation for buyers, corporations, and the planet as well. By traveling green, people help the Earth to be a cleaner place.

Chapter 4

Is Greener Really Cleaner?

Twenty-five-year-old Justin loves his Saturn sedan. But he does not love what it does to the environment. Justin knows that his car spews carbon dioxide gas into the air. This gas causes pollution. It also traps heat from the Sun. Both of these effects are bad for the Earth.

Justin thinks he knows a way to reduce his car's impact. Each year he sends money to a business called TerraPass. TerraPass invests the money in companies that are working to clean up the atmosphere. Justin is therefore paying to take pollution out of the air. If he pays enough money, he can "clean up" more pollution than his car caused. In green terms, the car is now carbon neutral. This term does not mean that Justin's car is pollution free. It means that Justin has canceled out his car's impact.

Justin knows it would be better if he just stopped driving. But he needs his car. He feels that TerraPass lets him drive and be green at the same time. "It would be incredibly difficult for me to [cut] those

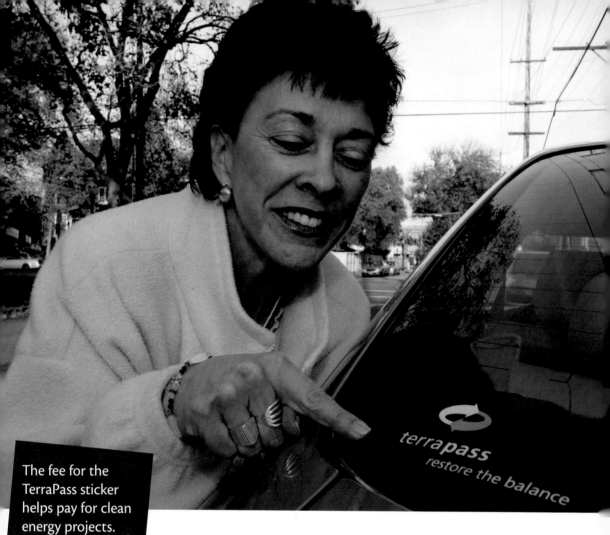

The fee for the TerraPass sticker helps pay for clean energy projects.

emissions now, yet I feel responsible to. This is a way for me to work toward doing that,"[22] he says.

The Carbon Question

Justin's car might be carbon neutral. But Justin himself still has a long way to go. Every day he air-conditions his home and watches TV. He turns on lightbulbs. He eats food that has been shipped long distances to the store. These daily activities plus many others release carbon dioxide into the air. Together, they make up Justin's carbon footprint.

Every person has a carbon footprint. Like Justin, many people try to erase their footprints by investing in green businesses. This act is called buying carbon offsets. It is a popular concept in the green movement today. TerraPass and many other companies sell offsets—and millions of people are

As Green As They Seem?

Trends are not always as green as they seem. Here are a few big questions in the green movement.

- Ethanol: Sure, it is better to burn corn than fossil fuels. But ethanol pollutes the air almost as much as gas does. Also, turning corn into gas keeps it from being used as food. This causes problems for grocers and consumers.
- Cloth diapers: They keep disposable diapers out of landfills. However, they must be washed each time they are soiled. This takes energy. Studies show that cloth diapers actually have a higher carbon footprint than disposables.
- Organic foods: Chemical-free crops often have a low yield. An organic field might produce just half the food of a traditional one. Critics therefore complain that organics waste precious farmland.

buying. Even the Queen of England takes part. In 2007 she paid $20,000 to offset her plane's carbon during one U.S. trip.

Offset buyers are proud of their choices. They feel that they are helping the Earth. Some people, however, do not see things this way. They think offsets encourage bad habits. One man explains it with these words: "I'm not a fan of this carbon offsetting business. It seems like a cop-out. So people with money can live however they want, then claim to be 'green' by paying a fee. If you want to produce less carbon, you should actually produce less carbon,"[23] he says.

Other people dislike offsets for different reasons. They point out that carbon reduction is very hard to prove. They worry that offset payments go into someone's pocket, not into environmental work. "There's a lot of that happening: buying offsets that aren't really real,"[24] says one industry expert.

How Green Is It?

This person raises a good point. Businesses today want to be seen as green. They are selling more and more things that claim to be Earth friendly. But are these claims true? It can be hard to tell. For buyers, green labels do not always equal green products.

Cosmetics seller Clairol provides an example of the problem. In 2002 the company said that its Herbal Essences shampoos offered "a truly organic experience." The products did have some organic ingredients. But they also contained harmful

Wal-Mart is one of many companies accused of greenwashing.

chemicals and dyes. Critics therefore felt that Clairol was lying to the public. They said the company was greenwashing. This term means falsely claiming to be green.

Retailer Wal-Mart is often accused of greenwashing, too. Today Wal-Mart sells natural shirts, pants, and more. These items are made of chemical-free organic cotton. Wal-Mart says this material is greener than regular cotton. However, some people point out that Wal-Mart's cotton is grown in China. It must be shipped around the world to reach U.S.

stores. This causes pollution in the process. In other words, Wal-Mart is just swapping one kind of harm for another.

Clairol and Wal-Mart are not alone. Many other businesses have been accused of greenwashing. Auto and oil companies are particular targets. Many of these companies work hard to improve the Earth's health. But in critics' eyes, this work does not count. As long as these companies sell harmful goods, say some, they can never be green.

Going Green Is Good Business

These examples show that any green claim can be questioned. Still, companies are trying to keep things clean. Today a lot of businesses are doing a lot of good for the environment.

Kufala Recordings is one of these businesses. This company uses Earth-friendly shrink wrap on its CDs. It was not cheap to develop this product. But Kufala owner Brady Lahr does not mind the cost. He thinks going green is good business. "Every day you turn on the news, there's something about . . . ways to make the world a greener place. If we're not doing that in business, we're not looking out for the interest of our customer, which is the number-one priority in any business,"[25] he says.

Small companies can afford to go green for moral reasons. But big ones cannot. They must make money if they want to survive. So when they go green, they do it very carefully. Home Depot, for instance, launched its Eco Options line partly to keep its customers from straying. "Once we get someone hooked on Eco Options, why would they go to another store that doesn't offer something similar? It's about choice,"[26] says one Home Depot executive.

The issue, of course, is not just about cash. Most big companies truly want to do the right thing. To make it happen, many are asking for advice. Coca-Cola, Dell Computers, McDonald's, and Wal-Mart

Workers ride bikes and rainwater is used to flush toilets at a new, green General Motors factory.

are just a few of the companies working with green advisers today.

This situation is a huge step forward for the green movement. Not long ago, big business was seen as the enemy. Now it is a partner. "Companies have decided it is better to invite us into the tent than have us outside picketing," explains one green leader. "It's a long way from where we started."[27]

Will It Make a Difference?

The green movement may have come a long way. But many people feel that it has not come nearly far enough. They think individuals should try hard-

The Lazy Environmentalist

Which products are really green and which are just unclean? A radio show called *The Lazy Environmentalist* tries to sort out the claims. Host Josh Dorfman talks about green products and services. He also speaks with people who are active in the green movement. By doing so, he helps his listeners to make green choices.

Dorfman's show airs weekdays on Sirius satellite radio. His advice also appears in a book called *The Lazy Environmentalist*. The book itself, of course, is Earth friendly. It is printed on recycled, bleach-free paper.

In good weather, this New York man rides his bike almost everywhere.

er. "I am appalled at what my high school friends do and what they don't perceive to be a problem,"[28] says a young man named Mobius.

As Mobius points out, some people simply do not see the problem. Others, however, see it very well. Still, they do nothing. They say that the Earth is in too much trouble. They think that one person cannot make a difference. Therefore they do not even try to change their lives.

Environmentalists do not agree with this approach. They say that many people together *can* make a difference. One good example, they say, is lightbulb usage. If everyone in America used just one compact fluorescent lightbulb, it would be like taking millions of cars off the road.

Businesses can have a big impact, too. Wal-Mart, for instance, recently designed smaller boxes for one line of toys. This change will save about 5,000 trees each year. Because trucks can now hold more toys, it will also cut pollution. For Wal-Mart this was a very small effort. In green terms, however, the results were huge. This story shows how easy it can be to make Earth-friendly decisions.

There are big problems to overcome, of course. Carbon dioxide continues to pollute the air. Trash keeps going into landfills. People keep using more power than they need. To make matters worse, the Earth's population is growing. Every new person adds another burden to the planet. It is easy to become overwhelmed by these facts.

Giving up, however, is not the answer. People need to look at what they can do, not what they cannot do. Then they should do it. By taking baby steps, people can slowly heal the Earth— or at least stop hurting it. One blogger puts it this way:

> Green goes beyond purchasing the right home and making sure we are not surrounded by toxins. Green is loving ourselves and our neighbor enough to limit our . . . consumption. . . . Green is appreciating the earth that surrounds us. . . . Green is opening the windows. . . . Green is walking the

Painting Hollywood Green

Many famous actors are going green. Leonardo DiCaprio is devoted to the cause. So is Woody Harrelson. Brad Pitt recently helped to build a green home in New Orleans, Louisiana. Cameron Diaz drives a Prius. And Ed Begley Jr. often bikes to red-carpet events.

Celebrities cannot clean up the world on their own. But they are having a big impact anyway. They are inspiring other people to take action. "Leonardo DiCaprio is not going to solve the problems. But if he gets people talking about it, that is good work on his part," says *Rolling Stone* editor Will Dana.

Quoted in *ABC World News*, "What's Hot in Hollywood? Going Green," January 10, 2007. http://abcnews.go.com/GMA/GlobalWarming/Story?id=2781681&page=1.

Things You Can Do to Help the Planet

Adopt something – An animal, a stream, a whale	
Avoid fast food – This helps reduce waste. Most fast food is wrapped in too much packaging.	
Bike instead of ride – This saves energy and reduces pollution.	
Buy products made of recycled paper	
Change a lightbulb	
Clean up a stream or park	
Close the refrigerator door	
Collect aluminum cans and recycle	
Create a compost pile	
Donate your toys to a worthy cause	
Don't buy aerosols – These include products like hairspray.	
Eat organic produce	
Plant a tree	
Recycle batteries – Do not throw them away. They become hazardous waste.	
Turn off lights	

Source: www.geocities.com/RainForest/Vines/4990/.

neighborhood, not always driving it. . . . Green is evaluating how we use energy. . . . Green is about the little things, because everyone's little bit counts. [29]

This person is right. Every little bit does count. By taking small actions, each person can help to make the world a healthier place.

Notes

Introduction: Why Go Green?

1. Quoted in Eric Horng, "Ditching Bottled Water to Go Green," *ABC World News*, Sunday, July 8, 2007.
2. Quoted in Dan Eggen, "Earth Day Crowd Targets Global Warming," *Washington Post*, April 23, 2000. http://commondreams.org/headlines/042300-02.htm.

Chapter 1: Going Green at Home

3. Quoted in CBC.ca, "Shades of Green." www.cbc.ca/ottawa/features/goingforgreen/.
4. Quoted in CBC.ca, "Shades of Green."
5. Quoted in Christine Maddox, "Composting Is an Ideal Way to Aid the Environment," *SpringfieldNewsSun.com*, August 4, 2007. www.springfieldnewssun.com/green/content/oh/story/living/2007/2007/08/03/ddn080407lifecomposting.html.
6. Quoted in BBC News, "Talking Point: Do You Buy Organic Food?" June 23, 2000. http://news.bbc.co.uk/1/hi/talking_point/790811.stm.

7. Quoted in OrganicAuthority.com, "The Cotton Club." www.organicauthority.com/organic-living/organic-living/the-cotton-club.html.

8. Dorothy Foltz-Gray, "*Health*'s Guide to Going Green," *Health*, April 2007, p. 108.

9. Quoted in Ryan Bentley, "Petoskey Schools Going to Green Cleaning Products," *Petoskey (MI) News-Review*, September 5, 2007. www.petoskeynews.com/articles/2007/09/05/news/news04.txt.

10. Quoted in Louisa Pearson, "Winds of Change," *Scotsman.com,* October 22, 2006. http://living.scotsman.com/index.cfm?id=1551032006.

Chapter 2: Building Green

11. Quoted in Marija Potkonjak, "Scottsdale Home Uses Efficient Technologies," *East Valley Tribune*, January 13, 2007. www.eastvalleytribune.com/story/82259.

12. Quoted in Potkonjak, "Scottsdale Home Uses Efficient Technologies."

13. Quoted in Mike Lee, "A Glimpse of the Future for 'Green' Construction," *San Diego Union-Tribune*, July 7, 2007. www.signonsandiego.com/uniontrib/20070707/news_1n7green.html.

14. Quoted in Debra Lynn Dadd, "Green Living Q&A: How Long Does Paint Outgas?" www.dld123.com/q&a/index.php?category=Air.

15. Quoted in Louisa Pearson, "Winds of Change."

16. Quoted in Alana Klein, "Green Expectations," *University Business*, February 2005, p. 52.

Chapter 3: Getting Around in Green Style

17. Quoted in Jerry Adler, "Going Green," *Newsweek*, July 17, 2006.

18. Quoted in Hybrid Answers, "How Could You Help the Environment and Global Warming w/o Changing Too Much of Normal Habits?" http://jporchanian.wordpress.com/2007/08/26/how-could-you-help-the-environment-and-global-warming-wo-changing-too-much-of-normal-habits/.

19. Tom Carter, "Why I Bought a Prius," Eat at Tom's, January 27, 2004. www.home.earthlink.net/~tomecarter/index.html.

20. Quoted in Marianne Schnall, "Interview with Ed Begley, Jr.," EcoMall. www.ecomall.com/greenshopping/ed.htm.

21. Quoted in NASA Explores, "Wanted: Green Airplanes," March 29, 2001. www.nasaexplores.com/search_nav_9_12.php?id=01-021&gl=912.

Chapter 4: Is Greener Really Cleaner?

22. Quoted in Warren Cornwall, "For Sale: CO_2 by the Ton," *Seattle Times*, November 13, 2006. http://seattletimes.nwsource.com/html/localnews/2003415416_carbon13m.html.

23. Quoted in Environmental Economics, "Guilt-Free Travel," June 30, 2006. www.env-econ.net/2006/06/guiltfree_trave.html.

24. Quoted in Cornwall, "For Sale."
25. Quoted in Todd Martens, "Down to Earth,"
   Billboard, June 23, 2007, p. 29.
26. Quoted in Mya Frazier, "Going Green? Plant
   Deep Roots," *Advertising Age*, April 30, 2007.
   www.adage.com.
27. Quoted in John Carey, "Hugging the Tree-
   Huggers," *Business Week*, March 12, 2007. www.
   businessweek.com/magazine/content/07_11/b4
   025076.htm.
28. Quoted in TreeHugger Forums, "Are Younger
   Generations Going Green?" July 5, 2007. http://
   forums.treehugger.com/viewtopic.php?t=864.
29. Lola Audu, "Green Confessions of a 'Gen Y'
   Mom," Active Rain Real Estate Network.
   http://activerain.com/blogsview/55743/Green-
   Confessions-of-a.

Glossary

biofuel: Fuel made from plant or animal by-products.

carbon footprint: The total amount of carbon dioxide given off by a person, product, or service.

carbon neutral: Removing carbon dioxide from the atmosphere equal to the amount added.

carbon offset: An action that reduces, or "pays for," carbon added to the atmosphere. People buy carbon offsets to cancel their carbon footprints.

composting: The controlled breakdown of organic matter to produce soil.

disposable: An item that is meant to be thrown away after one use.

greenwashing: Claiming that an action or product is greener than it really is.

landfill: A site where solid waste is dumped and treated or stored.

organic: Produced without using chemical fertilizers, pesticides, or drugs.

renewable: Easily replaced by natural processes.

volatile organic compounds (VOCs): Fume-producing chemicals found in traditional paints, stains, glues, and other building materials.

Bibliography

Books

Will Anderson, *Diary of an Eco-builder*. Devon, England: Green Books, 2006. This book tells the story of one man's attempt to build a green home.

Philippe Bourseiller, *365 Ways to Save the Earth*. New York: Abrams, 2005. This lovely book includes 365 photos of the Earth's wildest places, along with suggestions for saving them.

Laurie David and Cambria Gordon, *The Down-to-Earth Guide to Global Warming*. New York: Orchard, 2007. Is carbon dioxide really heating up the Earth? This book summarizes the arguments on both sides of this issue.

Caroline Kettlewell, *Electric Dreams: One Unlikely Team of Kids and the Race to Build the Car of the Future*. New York: Carroll & Graf, 2004. This book tells the true story of a high school team that entered a contest to convert a regular car into an electric vehicle.

Debra A. Miller, *Organic Foods*. Detroit: Lucent, 2007. This book takes a close-up look at the organic foods industry.

Nicky Scott, *Composting: An Easy Household Guide*. White River Junction, VT: Chelsea Green, 2007. This how-to book includes basic information on composting.

Crissy Trask, *It's Easy Being Green: A Handbook for Earth-Friendly Living.* Salt Lake City: Gibbs Smith, 2006. This day-to-day guide for green living includes lots of easy, practical suggestions.

Web Sites

Ecological Footprint Quiz (www.myfootprint.org). Use this site's calculator to find your carbon footprint.

GE Ecomagination (http://ge.ecomagination.com/site/index.html). Learn about some of the cool green things General Electric is developing.

Greenpeace USA (www.greenpeace.org/usa). Greenpeace fights for the environment in countless ways. This Web site communicates the group's actions and beliefs.

An Inconvenient Truth (www.climatecrisis.net). This is the official Web site of the movie. It summarizes many of the issues discussed in the film.

The Lazy Environmentalist (www.lazyenvironmentalist.com). This Web site complements the radio show and book of the same name.

TreeHugger (www.treehugger.com). This site covers every aspect of the green movement. It includes forums where teens can chat about green issues.

Index

Picture Credits

Cover photo: AP Images
Maury Aaseng, 15, 18, 52
AP Images/Alex Brandon, 22
AP Images/Harry Cabluck, 12
AP Images/EyePress, 29
AP Images/Kevin W. Fowler, 47
AP Images/Jennifer Graylock, 8
AP Images/John Heupel, 49
AP Images/Jae C. Hong, 20
AP Images/Matt Houston, 50
AP Images/Lawrence Jackson, 25
AP Images/Katsumi Kasahara, 40
AP Images/Leslie E. Kossoff, 33
AP Images/Kelley McCall, 26
AP Images/Paul Sakuma, 5, 45
AP Images/Marcio Jose Sanchez, 42
AP Images/Tim Sharp, 27
AP Images/Paul Skipper, 32
AP Images/Jan-Michael Stump, 38
AP Images/Tony Talbot, 36
BananaStock/JupiterImages Unlimited, 9
Creatas Images/JupiterImages, 14
© Charlotte Thege/Alamy, 11

Kris Hirschmann has written more than 170 books for children. She owns and runs The Wordshop (www.the-wordshop.com), a business that provides a variety of writing and editorial services. Hirschmann lives just outside Orlando, Florida, with her husband, Michael, and her daughters, Nikki and Erika.